SAHARA WEST

D0568097

THAILAND

GROLIER

An Imprint of Scholastic Library Publishing
Danbury, Connecticut

Published for Grolier,
an imprint of Scholastic Library Publishing
Old Sherman Turnpike, Danbury, Connecticut 06816
by Times Editions,
an imprint of Times Media Pte Ltd

Set ISBN: 0-7172-5788-6
Volume ISBN: 0-7172-5803-3

Library of Congress Cataloging-in-Publication Data
Thailand.
p. cm.—(Fiesta!)
Summary: Discusses the festivals and holidays of Thailand and how the songs, food,
and traditions associated with these celebrations reflect the culture of the people.
1. Festivals—Thailand—Juvenile literature. 2. Thailand—Social life and customs—Juvenile literature.
[1. Festivals—Thailand. 2. Holidays—Thailand. 3. Thailand—Social life and customs.]
I. Grolier (Firm). II. Fiesta! (Danbury, Conn.)
GT4878.A2T36   2004
394.26593—dc21   2003044853

For this volume
Author: Cyril Wong
Editor: Yeo Puay Khoon
Designer: Christopher Wong
Production: Nor Sidah Haron
Crafts and Recipes produced by Stephen Russell

Printed in Malaysia

Adult supervision advised for all crafts and recipes,
particularly those involving sharp instruments and heat.

CONTENTS

THAILAND

Set in the very heart of Southeast Asia, Thailand is also known as the land of smiles. This tropical country has a population of over 60 million and is nearly the size of France.

▼ **Bangkok**, the capital, is a well-known tourist spot. It is the largest city in Thailand, and it is the center for the government, business, and royalty. The Grand Palace was built in 1782 as the official residence of the king. Today, the palace is used for certain ceremonial occasions such as Coronation Day.

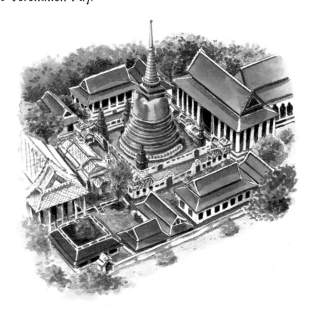

▲ **Temples** are known as *wat* in Thai. Temples in the cities tend to be huge, while temples in rural villages are small and modest. They are places for religious ceremonies and meditation.

4

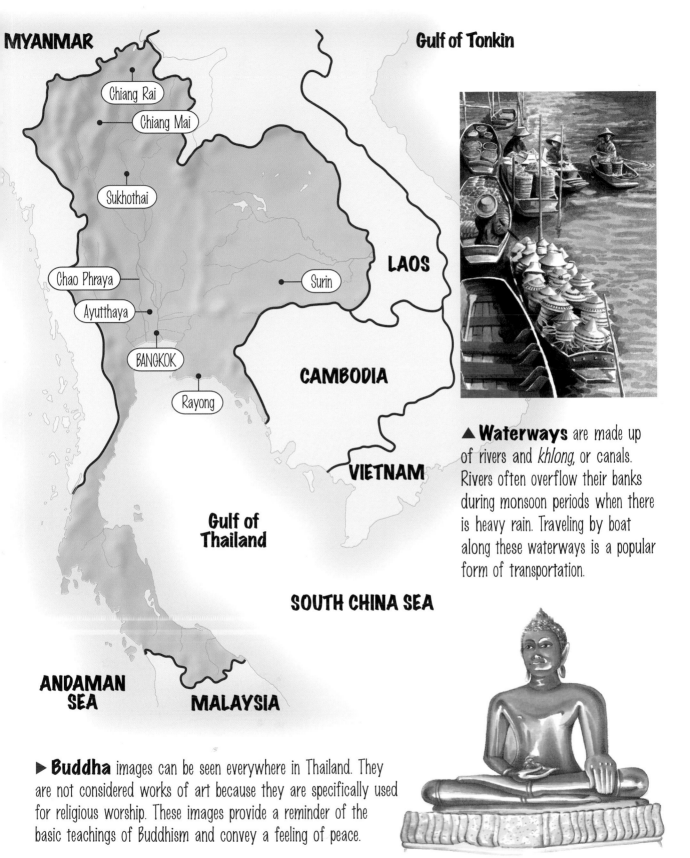

MYANMAR

Gulf of Tonkin

Chiang Rai

Chiang Mai

Sukhothai

LAOS

Chao Phraya

Ayutthaya

Surin

BANGKOK

CAMBODIA

Rayong

VIETNAM

Gulf of
Thailand

SOUTH CHINA SEA

ANDAMAN
SEA

MALAYSIA

▲ **Waterways** are made up of rivers and *khlong,* or canals. Rivers often overflow their banks during monsoon periods when there is heavy rain. Traveling by boat along these waterways is a popular form of transportation.

▶ **Buddha** images can be seen everywhere in Thailand. They are not considered works of art because they are specifically used for religious worship. These images provide a reminder of the basic teachings of Buddhism and convey a feeling of peace.

RELIGIONS

The most popular religion in Thailand is Buddhism. Thailand is probably the country with the largest number of Buddhist followers in the world.

BUDDHISM IS THOUSANDS of years old. It was founded by Siddhartha Gotama, who is also known as Lord Buddha. The followers of Buddhism are called Buddhists.

As a result of the Buddhist idea that life will pass away and that one should be at peace

A statue of Buddha in the teaching mudra.

with oneself, Thai people are often relaxed and carefree.

Buddhist places of worship are called temples or shrines. At such places monks teach the rules of human conduct laid down by Buddha more than two thousand five hundred years ago. These monks live in the wat, which is a walled monastery.

The wat is the center of communal life in the villages, where monks serve as doctors and psychologists as well as judges during disputes between villagers. Monks also give blessings to buildings that have just been built and also at birthdays and funerals.

Thai tradition requires that every Buddhist male enters monkhood for a period of between seven days and six months. Some men even become monks permanently.

Before the Buddhist male is ordained to be a monk, his head is shorn of all hair. While in the temple, he listens to sermons based on Buddha's teachings and meditates frequently.

There are images of Buddha all

over the country. The images of Buddha have certain postures called *mudra*. For example, the most popular image of Buddha sitting with both hands in his lap is called the meditation mudra.

The holy day of the week in Buddhism is called *wan phra*, a day determined by the lunar calendar. During this day Thais go to the wat to listen to monks chant scriptures and deliver sermons.

GREETINGS FROM **THAILAND!**

Most of Thailand is rural and made up of rice fields, plantations, and forests. The official language is Thai. It originated in the hills of southern Asia, where the Thai people first appeared, and has Indian influences. From the languages of India have come names and words with many syllables. As a result, Thai names are among the longest in the world. One of the most charming aspects of Thai culture is the *wai*, the gesture of greeting and parting. The wai is essentially the pressing together of palms, accompanied by a nod of the head, a slight bow, and the Thai hello: Sa Wat Dee.

How do you say...

Hello (women say this)
Sa wat dee ka

Hello (men say this)
Sa wat dee kup

How are you
Sa baay dee reuu

Thank you (women say this)
Kha poon ka

Thank you (men say this)
Kha poon kup

Never mind
Mai pen rai

MAKHA PUJA

This holiday falls on a full-moon day in the third lunar month, usually February. During this day it is a time to strengthen one's faith in Buddha and also to do good deeds.

Buddha in the meditation mudra under a Bodhi tree.

Since Thailand is made up of people who are mostly Buddhists, many Buddhist festivals are celebrated in the country. Makha Puja is considered one of the holiest days in Buddhism. During this time it is important to avoid bad actions and to purify one's mind.

It was on this day many years ago when 1,250 Buddhists paid homage to Buddha. Seeing that all these disciples had come to him, Buddha delivered his great sermon, called the *Patimokha*. These disciples, also called *Arahantas*, were followers of Buddhism who had already been Enlightened. This means that they completely understood the nature of life. The Patimokha is a set of daily observances found in Buddhism. It consists of a set of rules made by Buddha to ensure peace and well-being within the community. These rules were also made to protect the faith of the common people on whom the

Three joss sticks are offered together with a candle and lotus flowers to express devotion.

procession, called Wien Tien, in the evening.

The celebration of Makha Puja truly follows Buddha's advice to his followers that if they are to thrive, they should meet together regularly and in large numbers.

Festivals like Makha Puja are opportunities for Buddhists to celebrate and express their devotion and thanks to Buddha and his teachings. Also, it is a time for "merit-making."

Merit-making refers to the doing of good deeds in order to gain spiritual rewards. It is believed that, through merit-making, people can eventually acquire enough merit so that they attain Nirvana, which is the state of spiritual enlightenment.

monks depended on for support. Altogether there are 227 rules in the Patimokha. These rules are formally recited twice a month in every monastery in Thailand.

Makha Puja was first celebrated in Thailand at the Temple of the Emerald Buddha in 1851. Since then the ceremony has been performed throughout the kingdom. People from all walks of life visit the temple to perform religious activities in the morning. There is also a candlelit

People make offerings of fruit to Buddhist monks for merit-making.

SONGKRAN FESTIVAL

This festival take place between April 13 and 15. It marks the start of the Thai New Year.

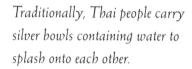

Songkran comes from an old Sanskrit word meaning "Beginning of the Solar Year."

The people of Thailand celebrate two new years. The first New Year is on January 1, just as in most countries. The other Thai New Year is called the Songkran.

It is also referred to as "The Start of the Returns of the Rains" or simply as "Thai New Year." The Thais spring-clean their houses thoroughly before the celebrations. All homes are cleaned on the eve of the festival, and anything old or broken is thrown out so that it will not bring bad luck. Buddha images are bathed as part of the ceremony. On Songkran day offerings are made at Buddhist temples.

Children show their respect to elders by performing the water ceremony, pouring water slowly into the palms of their parents and the hands of older relatives. People release caged animals at this time and give food to monks as ways of merit-making. Families have a get-together during this time.

It may seem like a peaceful event, but over the years the Songkran water-splashing ritual has become a huge fun-filled water-fight. In the streets people splash water on

Traditionally, Thai people carry silver bowls containing water to splash onto each other.

one another.

This goes on all day from dawn until dusk. It is a good-natured celebration, with almost everybody joining in. People fill the backs of pickup trucks with huge containers of water, buckets, and water

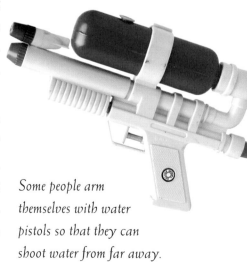

Some people arm themselves with water pistols so that they can shoot water from far away.

cannons and join a slow-moving procession through the streets. Friends and family members stand atop the trucks and splash water onto passers-by along the streets. The water-splashing is all done in the name of good fun, and even uniformed policemen will gladly get wet!

The age-old custom of throwing water is thought to have been derived from a rainmaking ceremony. *Nagas* were mythical serpents that were thought to have brought rain by spouting water from the seas. The more water they spouted, the more rain fell on the land. That is why

Thais throw water during the Songkran festival.

Fish are released back into the rivers for merit-making.

MAKE A SPIRIT HOUSE

A spirit house is a small makeshift house that stands in the grounds of most buildings in Thailand. Some resemble temples, while others are models of houses. Thai people believe that guardian spirits live in the spirit house, and every day they bring the spirits offerings of fresh food, flowers, and incense. These spirits are supposed to grant protection to the place where the spirit house sits.

YOU WILL NEED
1 cardboard box
1 piece of rectangular cardboard
PVA glue
Masking tape
Color paint
Newspapers
Water

1 Draw a pair of doors on one side of the cardboard box. Ask an adult to help you cut the doors so that they can open and close.

2 Fold the piece of cardboard in half to form a steep roof, and attach it to the box with masking tape. Decorate the house by cutting patterns to line the roof.

3 Tear newspapers into 1 inch squares, and mix them in a bowl of PVA glue and water to create papier-mâché. Paste the papier-mâché all over the house.

4 Let the papier-mâché dry. Once the papier-mâché is dry, paint your house in any color you like.

Spirit houses are usually elevated on poles and placed outside buildings in Thailand.

ROYAL PLOWING CEREMONY

For more than seven hundred years this annual event has taken place in early May at the Grand Palace in Bangkok. The ancient rite is held to produce bountiful harvests and to boost the morale of farmers.

The growing of rice is essential to the livelihood and economy of Thailand. The majority of Thai people are rice farmers.

The Plowing Ceremony originated in India, and it has been passed down to Thailand over the years. This ceremony is important to Thai farmers, since it helps determine how much rain will fall and how well their crops will grow.

At the beginning of the ceremony the Lord of the Festival performs a rite to predict the amount of rainfall during the coming season. He selects one out of three pieces of cloth, each of a different length. If the shortest one is chosen, rainfall will be abundant; rice in high areas will be plentiful, but rice in low areas may be flooded. If the medium cloth is picked, rainfall will be average, and rice abundant. If the long cloth is selected, rain will be scarce, and rice in low areas plentiful, but rice in high areas may suffer from drought.

The Lord then wears the piece of cloth and goes to the plowing area, paying his respects to his Majesty the King. The king plays an important role in these ceremonies. He

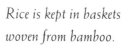

Rice is kept in baskets woven from bamboo.

drummers, and Brahmans chant alongside while blowing horns made of conch shells.

The bulls are unyoked after the plowing and then presented with rice seed, green beans, corn, hay, sesame seed, water, and rice liquor. What they eat or drink predicts the outcome of the growing season. For example, if rice seed or corn is selected, cereal and fruit will be bountiful.

Spectators rush onto the field after the ceremony and pick up the sacred rice grains. They are mixed with other rice seeds for planting or kept as holy items.

Green beans, red beans, and soya beans are some of the items presented to the bulls at the Plowing Ceremony.

oversees the traditional Plowing Ceremony that signifies the start of the rice-planting season. A pair of ceremonial bulls is yoked to a plow that is painted red and gold, while the bulls are covered with gold-colored cloth and tassels.

Using these bulls, the Lord of the Festival plows the land, scattering rice seeds from gold baskets carried by four women. As the field is being plowed, umbrella-bearers,

SPICY CUCUMBER SALAD

SERVES 4

¼ cup rice vinegar
¼ cup granulated sugar
1 ½ tbsp water
¼ tsp salt
¼ cup white onion, finely chopped
5 fresh mint leaves, chopped
½ tbsp fresh parsley, chopped
1 fresh red chili, seeded and thinly sliced
1 tbsp dry-roasted peanuts, chopped
1 medium cucumber, halved lengthwise, seeded, and thinly sliced

1 Combine vinegar, sugar, water, and salt in a medium bowl. Whisk until sugar dissolves.

2 Add cucumber, onion, mint, parsley, and chili. Toss until evenly coated.

3 Let it sit for 15 minutes. Garnish with peanuts, and serve.

ROCKET FESTIVAL

This festival takes place in the sixth lunar month, which usually falls in May. Huge homemade rockets are fired at the sky in the belief that this will encourage the production of rain for better crops.

The homemade rockets are decorated in bright colors to add to the festivities.

The Rocket Festival, or Boon Bang Fai in Thai, is usually held in the second week of May each year, at the beginning of the rainy season. At this time the rice farmers are ready to cultivate their fields. The celebration is an appeal to the rain god for rain during the rice planting season.

The festival owes its beginning to a legend that a rain god named Vassakan was known for his fascination with being worshipped with fire. To receive plentiful rain for rice cultivation, farmers send homemade rockets to the heavens where the god is known to live.

As at several other Thai festivals, Buddhist monks are present for the ceremony. The celebration involves placing huge homemade rockets on a 39-foot-tall bamboo launching pad. A very brave person lights the fuse, then runs away before the rocket ignites and swooshes skyward at amazing speeds.

The secrets of rocket making have been passed down over generations, and they have been refined over the years. Nowadays rockets are even packed with several pounds of gunpowder!

To make the Rocket Festival more fun, people compete to see who can make the most colorful, and highest-flying rocket.

In the afternoon of the festival day the rockets are lined up in a procession and carried to the launch site. The people dressed in colorful traditional costumes attract the attention of many onlookers, who line up all along the procession route. As each rocket

Matches are used to light the fuses on the homemade rockets.

is fired, spectators clap and cheer.

Those not involved in this celebration perform merit-making rituals. They pray, make offerings, and burn incense. In some parts of Thailand the festival may also involve singers wandering among the crowds singing songs throughout the day.

In addition, there are other activities to keep people occupied. They include live music, dancing, and contests

VISAKHA PUJA

This holiday falls on a full-moon day in May. It is the holiest of all Buddhist religious days, marking the birth, enlightenment, and death of Buddha.

Visakha Puja and Makha Puja have one thing in common. During these holy days temples throughout the country are crowded with people who come to listen to sermons by revered monks. In the evening

Temples are filled with people celebrating Visakha Puja.

there are solemn candlelit processions around major temples, and worshippers carry candles, incense, and flowers.

Visakha Puja is also known as Vesak Day. The date for it is determined according to the lunar calendar followed by Buddhists. All Buddhists commemorate Buddha's birth, enlightenment, and death on this day. These events take place on the full-moon day in May. They occur when the

moon appears in line with a group of stars called Visakha, which explains why this particular day is named Visakha Puja.

When this event is celebrated, Buddhists take the opportunity to pay homage to Buddha by expressing gratitude for his virtue. Houses are cleaned and decorated with garlands of flowers. Sand is taken from nearby river banks and spread over temple courtyards. Statues of Buddha are brought out of temples to be cleaned and polished. All religious scriptures also have to be dusted.

However, some daily activities stop so that people can take part in merit-making activities. It

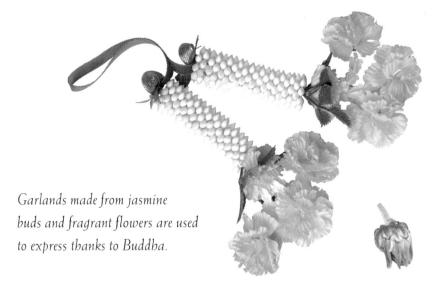

by performing activities such as deep meditation. It improves the spiritual development of the mind in the way that Buddha had taught.

Garlands made from jasmine buds and fragrant flowers are used to express thanks to Buddha.

is common on this day for Buddhists to practice generosity, observe the scriptures, and listen to *Dhamma*, the teachings of Buddha.

In addition, the people refrain from enjoying certain luxuries. Jewels, perfumes, and cologne are set aside on this day. They dress very simply, and they do not sleep on beds or mattresses when they rest. Also, instead of having three or four meals, they restrict themselves to only one or two meals that day.

Buddhists pay their greatest tribute to Buddha

THE STORY OF THE BUDDHA

Visakha Puja is a time when Buddhists remember and commemorate the Enlightenment of Buddha. The story of how he attained Enlightenment and his teachings inspire Buddhists all over the world.

MANY YEARS AGO in North India there lived a king called Suddhodana.

One night his wife Queen Maha Maya had a strange dream. She saw a huge white elephant come into her bedroom, carrying a lotus flower. The elephant trumpeted as it walked around her bed three times. When the wise men of the land heard about the dream, they proclaimed that a great and noble son would be born to the queen. The king and queen were very happy.

On their way to the queen's parents' home they had to pass a forest and some lovely gardens called Lumbini. When the queen arrived at this delightful place, she decided to rest for a while in the cool shade. While seated under a tree, she gave birth to a baby boy. It was the full-moon day in the month of Vesak. The baby was very beautiful. His skin was the color of gold, and his eyes were deep blue.

His hair was black, and his whole body was perfectly formed.

A wise sage called Asita visited the palace after the birth. He said that the baby would become the greatest king in history. If he did not become a king, he would become a Buddha, a fully Enlightened One, who would teach the whole world how to find true happiness and relief from sorrow.

The parents were stunned by this. The baby was named Siddhartha, which means "the One whose wishes will be fulfilled."

King Suddhodana ordered that only the happy and beautiful aspects of life should surround the prince. Old and sick people were kept out of his sight. Death was not mentioned. But the efforts of King Suddhodana to shield his son from sadness and suffering only increased the prince's curiosity to see the world outside. So, one

roadside. This was a very unusual sight for the prince. On another day when he was out, he saw a sick man. On his third visit he saw a funeral procession.

"I have learned that all living beings grow old and ugly, get ill, and die. I am sad when I think about all this," was Siddhartha's response to what he had seen. He swore he would seek a way to end suffering. He left the palace, exchanging all his beautiful clothes for those of a beggar. He went to well-known teachers of the time and studied very hard to be enlightened, so that he could be free of old age, illness, and death.

He starved himself, and tried many other ways to seek Enlightenment. One day he sat under the shade of a Bodhi tree and started to meditate. He resolved, "I will not move from here until I have attained full Enlightenment." He spent the whole evening in this meditation posture. Many thoughts came to distract him from his goal, but he was not deterred. With determination and willpower he continued to meditate until his mind became pure and clear. He emerged as the fully Enlightened One, or Buddha.

day he decided to take a walk outside the palace. He had not gone very far when he saw a hunched old man by the

BOAT RACING FESTIVALS

These festivals take place on chosen dates in September and October. Boat racing is a traditional event in Thailand and is considered a national sport today.

Traditional foods are enjoyed during the festive occasion.

Dancers wearing traditional dress, perform, and cheer on the competing boat racing teams.

For centuries the people have always traveled by boat along the many rivers and canals called *khlong* in Thailand. It is still a very convenient way of getting around the country.

Boat racing is a traditional event for the Thais, who are used to living by waterways. In September boat racing festivals are held in several provinces. Races are held on days when the river is the highest.

Although not restricted to any particular region, boat racing can be traced back some six hundred years to the province of Ayutthaya. At that time boat races were held to keep the young men fit. They helped train the men for war so that they were prepared for invasions.

Today, boat racing is considered a national sport. Boats are usually made out of a single large tree trunk. Oarsmen on the same team dress in the same brightly colored attire. The boats, built along the same lines as the original battle vessels, are decorated with ribbons and garlands of flowers.

As the boats race, people beat on drums to encourage the oarsmen. Professional announcers crack funny jokes during the competition. That makes the event plenty of fun. Sometimes there are even contests to see who is the best drum-beater! Other celebrations include decorative boat and team-cheering competitions.

COOL WATERMELON SLUSH

Thailand's tropical weather is usually hot, so there is nothing like a delicious slush to cool one down!

SERVES 4

6 ice cubes
Half a watermelon, cut into small
pieces and deseeded
1 tbsp of sugar or honey

1 Put the ice cubes in a blender or food processor. Ask an adult to blend the ice cubes until they are crushed.

2 Add the watermelon pieces, and blend for about 1 minute, or until the shake is slushy.

3 Add the sugar or honey, and blend for 10 seconds. Pour the slush into tall glasses, and serve.

TA-IN AND TA-NA

Thai people have lived near waterways for centuries. They depend on these waterways for food and transportation. "Ta-in and Ta-na" is a folk story set in this landscape of rivers and canals.

ONCE UPON A TIME there were two men who lived in the same coastal village.

One was named Ta-in, and the other was named Ta-na. They became good friends and did many things together. Ta-in and Ta-na were good fishermen, so they decided to fish together in the bay. They built a boat and caught lots of fish in the days that followed. They shared the fish they had caught and cooked them for their evening meal. After many months their luck began to change, and they caught fewer and fewer fish.

Very soon the two men had tried every place they knew to find fish but to no avail. Finally, Ta-in caught one, which they brought home. Since Ta-na had not caught a fish, Ta-in said that he would take the head and middle part of the fish and Ta-na could have the tail.

Ta-na did not like this. He also wanted the head and middle of the fish. But Ta-in shouted that it was not fair since he was the real owner of the fish because he had caught it. He deserved the head and middle, and Ta-na should be happy to take the tail. They could not agree and became angrier with each other. Finally they started to fight. Their fighting and loud shouts brought the villagers running.

A village elder called Ta-yoo pulled them apart and shouted, "Stop fighting!" Ta-in and Ta-na eventually calmed down. In the end, they agreed to let the elder solve their problem. Ta-yoo thought about the problem for a long time.

Finally he spoke. "Ta-in, you caught the fish, so you should take the head. Ta-na, you did not catch any fish, so you should take the tail. I am the one who has solved this problem, so I will take the middle part of the fish."

Both men were stunned. Since they could not think of any other solution, they had to agree to the elder's words. So Ta-in took the head, Ta-na picked up the tail,

and Ta-yoo took the biggest and best part of the fish – its middle. The villagers agreed that it was a fair solution and walked away.

Both Ta-in and Ta-na were very sad. "How foolish we were," said Ta-in. "I caught the fish, but Ta-yoo got the best part. I should not have been so selfish." "No, I was the selfish one," said Ta-na. "I didn't catch a fish, so I should have been happy to take the tail."

The two men looked at each other. They realized that they had both been greedy. They had ended up as losers because of their greed and selfishness. They had learned a valuable lesson.

From that day on they worked together and helped one another. They shared their catch no matter who had caught more fish. In time the fish returned again in great numbers, and Ta-in and Ta-na caught so many fish that they could sell most of them. They even hired other men to help them with their fishing. Besides becoming good friends again, they also became wealthy.

LOY KRATHONG

*On the full-moon night in November every river in Thailand is covered with hundreds of floating lanterns called **krathongs**. Thais believe that **krathongs** bring them good luck.*

During the night of Loy Krathong Thailand's rivers, *khlongs*, and hotel swimming pools are covered with blazing lights. This annual festival, also celebrated in neighboring countries, is held on the full-moon day of the twelfth lunar month. This event is of great importance to the Thais, and it is held all over the country.

The festival is believed to have started almost eight hundred years ago in Sukhothai Province, which lies in the northern part of the country. It was where the Thai king lived. When the rice fields were flooded and the rice had been sown, the farmers of Sukhothai held a festival of floating lanterns.

One day a beautiful woman named Nang Nophamat made some

special lotus-flower-shaped lanterns from banana leaves for the festival. The king was so impressed that he proclaimed that *krathongs* be floated on the river from then on.

"*Loy*" means to float, and "*krathong*" means a leaf cup. In most areas where it is celebrated, you will see Thai women in colorful attire with their flowers in their hair. Wherever there is water, colorfully dressed men and women gather with floats in their hands.

Coins are normally put in krathongs *for good luck.*

Most Thais believe the floating of the *krathong* is a way of removing past sins and bad luck. It is also believed that lovers can predict the future of their romance by watching their *krathongs* float downstream together.

November full-moon shine
Loy Krathong Loy Krathong
And the water high
In the gold river and the *khlong*

Loy Loy Krathong
Loy Loy Krathong
Loy Krathong is here
And everybody is full of cheer
We're together at the *klong*
Each one with his *krathong*
As we push away we pray
We can see a better day

The Loy Krathong festival is also a way to thank the goddess Mae Khongkha, the mother of water. That is because water is very precious to the Thai people, who depend on it for catching fish and growing rice.

LOY KRATHONG SONG

Wan Pen Du - an Sip Song Nam Koh Nong T - em Ta - ling Rao Tang - lai

Shai Ying Sa - nuk Gan - jing Wan Loy Krathong   Loy   Loy Kra - thong

Loy Loy Kra - thong Loy Kra - thong Gan Laew Koh Shern Nong Kaew Ook Ma Ram

Wong   Ra Wong Wan Loy Kra - thong Ram Wong Wan Loy Kra - thong Boon Ja

Song Hai Rao Suk Jai Boon Ja Song Hai Rao Suk Jai

MAKING A KRATHONG

*A **krathong** is a lotus-shaped vessel made of banana leaves. It usually contains a candle, three joss sticks, some flowers, and coins.*

YOU WILL NEED

Thin cardboard
Glue
Small candle
Plastic lid
Flowers with stems cut off
Incense sticks

1 Draw a large circle on the cardboard with a smaller circle inside. Draw petals between the two circles. Do this with two more pieces of cardboard so that you end up with three layers.

2 Cut out the layers, and fold up the petals. Arrange the layers on top of each other, and glue the bases together.

3 Ask an adult to help you cut a small cross in the center of the plastic lid, and push the candle through from the bottom so that it stands upright.

4 Place the lid in the center of the lotus, and insert the incense sticks. Arrange the flowers in the lotus so that they hide the lid.

ELEPHANT ROUNDUP

This festival takes place in Surin and is often held on the third weekend of November. Elephants dress in battle gear to pretend to go to war. The elephants even play soccer during this festival!

The people of Surin are well-known for their skill in capturing and training wild elephants. A *mahout* is a person trained to ride elephants. Elephants have been trained in Thailand for at least a thousand years. They help carry logs and heavy loads.

Elephants were used in battles and fought with their long, pointed tusks in order to defeat the enemy. In Thai art elephants appear everywhere – in paintings, on clothes, and in statues.

The greatest event of the Surin roundup is an organized display to show off the abilities of these impressive animals. The first roundup took place in 1960. The event begins with a procession of all the elephants taking part, usually between 120 and 150 of them. They range from calves, only a few weeks old, to well-trained elephants with many years of experience.

Elephants were used for war due to their strength and impressive size.

with the elephants during this procession.

During the show the

To joyously celebrate the elephant's special place in Thai culture, there are colorful gatherings of dancers and musicians in traditional dress together

huge animals demonstrate their skill in moving logs, playing soccer, and winning a tug-of-war against human teams. Although elephants are huge, they can be surprisingly fast and agile, as when they take part in soccer matches. The other demonstrations are planned to show their intelligence, gentleness, and obedience.

In the past the elephant roundup used to be an

THE ROYAL WHITE ELEPHANT

Since the thirteenth century the white elephant has been held in high regard and adopted as the emblem of the monarchy in Thailand. A white elephant has eyes, lips, nails, tail hair, skin, and hairs that are "close to white" in color. A law was passed in 1921 to ensure that any white elephants that are caught automatically belong to the king. So white elephants cannot be bought, sold, or used commercially. Keeping a white elephant is expensive, yet it cannot be used for work, so in the West the term "white elephant" is used to describe a possession that is useless and often expensive to maintain.

annual state ceremony presided over by the king. Since Thai culture is known for being very religious, there would also be prayers before the ceremony.

THE KING'S BIRTHDAY

An important public holiday is held on December 5 to celebrate the birthday of His Majesty King Bhumibol Adulyadej, the world's longest-reigning monarch.

Known in Thai as Wan Chalerm, the King's Birthday is marked by an outpouring of love and reverence by Thai people throughout the kingdom. It is the day that the people of Thailand express their gratitude, appreciation, and loyalty to the leadership of their king.

Although the king leads a busy life, he travels all over the country to help his people and continues to perform the ancient ceremonies of the kingdom.

Probably no other monarch in the world can truly claim to have so sincerely earned his people's love and respect. The king is also a talented poet, musician, engineer, painter, artist, as well as a skillful politician.

His Majesty King Bhumibol Adulyadej, or King Rama IX, ascended the throne on June 9, 1946.

On the king's birthday buildings and homes all over Thailand are decorated with flags, portraits of His Majesty, and bunting, a light, woolen cloth that is mostly yellow.

Thousands of vividly colored marigold flowers decorate the streets of Bangkok. The area around the Grand Palace is also spectacularly illuminated.

On the evening of the holiday itself many streets are closed to traffic, and thousands of people take to the streets. Spectacular fireworks displays are held, and the atmosphere is joyous and festive. Boat races may also be held in his honor. There are also stage shows and movies on giant screens for the people to enjoy. The official celebration in Bangkok includes a parade that is shown on television.

The sailing of the king's royal barge along the rivers of Bangkok is part of the birthday celebrations.

WORDS TO KNOW

Arahantas: Enlightened followers of Buddhism.

Brahman: A member of the highest level of Hindu society. They serve as priests in the royal court of Thailand.

Conch shells: Brightly colored spiral marine shells used as horns or ornaments.

Devotion: Profound dedication, especially to religion

Dhamma: The teachings of Buddha.

Lotus: A type of water lily that represents the purity of Buddha's enlightenment.

Merit-making: Doing good deeds in return for spiritual rewards.

Mudra: Attitudes, postures, or gestures seen in the images of Buddha.

Nagas: Spirits in the form of snakes, dragons, or cobras, known to bring rain.

Nirvana: A state of spiritual enlightenment.

Ordained: Fixed or established, especially by order or command.

Patimokha: A strict set of daily observances found in Buddhism.

Refrain: To hold oneself back.

Reverence: A feeling of profound awe and respect and often love.

Sanskrit: An ancient language from India that is the language of Hinduism.

Tassels: A bunch of loose threads or cords bound at one end and hanging free at the other, used as an ornament on curtains or clothing, for example.

Wai: Traditional Thai way of greeting and parting.

Wan Phra: Buddhist holy day of the week.

ACKNOWLEDGMENTS

WITH THANKS TO:
Alan Tay, Eric Koh, Anita Teo, and Lim Swee Hong for the loan of artifacts.

PHOTOGRAPHS BY:
Haga Library, Japan (cover), David Yip (p. 6), Yu Hui Ying (all other pictures)

ILLUSTRATIONS BY:
Enrico Sallustio (p. 1, pp. 4-5, p. 7), Lee Kowling (p. 19), Ong Lay Keng (p. 24), Amy Ong (p. 30)

SET CONTENTS